Mr. Ferlinghetti's Poem

Story and Woodcuts
by
David Frampton

Original poem
by
Lawrence Ferlinghetti

Eerdmans Books for Young Readers
Grand Rapids, Michigan • Cambridge, U.K.

Mr. Ferlinghetti remembers

a long hot summer in

Brooklyn

when he was a kid.

Mr. Ferlinghetti remembers

lots of things —

sad things,

happy things,

long ago things.

Sometimes Mr. Ferlinghetti
writes a poem about the things
he remembers. He wrote one
about that day, that steamy hot day
when he and Molly sat on the
stoop sighing through a
ho-hum summer.

Here is
          Mr. Ferlinghetti's

                    poem,

          just the way he wrote it.

Fortune
has its cookies to give out

which is a good thing

since it's been a long time since

that summer in Brooklyn
when they closed off the street
one hot day
and the

turned on their hoses

and all the kids ran out in it

in the middle of the street

and there were

maybe a couple dozen of us

out there

with the water squirting up

to the sky

and all over

us

there was maybe only six of us

                  kids altogether

   running around in our

            barefeet and birthday

suits

and I remember Molly but then
the firemen stopped squirting their hoses
all of a sudden and went
back in
their firehouse
and

started playing pinochle again
just as if nothing
had ever
happened

while I remember Molly

looked at me and

ran in

because I guess really we
were the only ones there